For Willia...
Plenty love

When September Comes

AND OTHER POEMS

Thanks for your
support
Peter Jailall
Sept 21/03

Peter Jailall

NATURAL HERITAGE BOOKS
TORONTO

Published by Natural Heritage / Natural History Inc.
P.O. Box 95, Station O, Toronto, Ontario M4A 2M8

www.naturalheritagebooks.com

National Library of Canada Cataloguing in Publication

Jailall, Peter, 1944-
    When September comes and other poems / Peter Jailall.

ISBN 1-896219-83-7

I.   Title.

PS8569.A414W54 2003   C811'.54   C2003-903575-1

Cover and text design by Derek Chung
Front Cover Photograph: Ralph Newton Photography
Edited by Melissa Hughes
Printed and bound in Canada by Hignell Book Printing, Winnipeg, Manitoba

Canada

Le Conseil des Arts | The Canada Council
du Canada | for the Arts
depuis 1957 | since 1957

ONTARIO ARTS COUNCIL
CONSEIL DES ARTS DE L'ONTARIO

Natural Heritage / Natural History Inc. acknowledges the financial support of the Canada Council for the Arts and the Ontario Arts Council for our publishing program. We acknowledge the support of the Government of Ontario through the Ontario Media Development Corporation's Ontario Book Initiative. We also acknowledge the financial support of the Government of Canada through the Book Publishing Industry Development Program (BPIDP) and the Association for the Export of Canadian Books.

Dedication

In memory of my grandparents: Mohabir (godfather) Bhudni (Miss Lil) Ramrattan (Hollan) and Rajwantie (Brownie).

Contents

Introduction

In this book of poems, I continue to engage in the search for the place called home on my journey to full Canadian citizenship. Although Guyana, "ole" country of my birth, has become violent and full of terror, pleasant memories of my birthplace continue to linger in my mind. Canada is my present home, but I have been returning to teach in Guyana since 1987. Like many new Canadians, I feel safe and somewhat settled in this landscape where I can go to sleep with an open door. But post September 11th, none of us can return to feelings of absolute security—suddenly we are all living under open, dangerous skies. These poems illustrate my journey to become both a Canadian and a global citizen with many identities, while celebrating the beauty of the natural environment in both of my homelands. I can't return to the Guyana of my childhood, but through my poems I'm able to explore the cultural and political tensions between past and present, East and West, and how these changes manifest in myself and my search for identity. In the same sense, I hope to challenge my readers, generally, and especially those in positions of authority, to look for change within and work for peace and justice in our world.

Acknowledgements

I would like to thank Dave and Nari, my sons, for assisting me on the computer and for their patience in getting the manuscript typed. I'm grateful to Sabi Jailall, my peer, partner and *dharam patni* for proofreading. Thanks to Chris Worsnop and especially Melissa Hughes for editing. And finally, thanks to Uncle Chabie Ramcharan for assistance with Hindi.

Peter Jailall

You Must be Born Again

Power on the airwaves. Power on the waterways. Power from the fighter plane. You must be born again. No more planets to find. You must be born again. No more oceans to cross. You must be born again. No more bodies to trade. You must be born again. No more diamonds to dig. You must be born again. No more cotton to pick. You must be born again. No more whipping and pain. You must be born again. Power on the airwaves. Children die. Power on the waterways. Mothers die. Power from the fighter plane.

You must be born again.

The Guyanese Roll Call

Listen to our roll call
of those who died
on that dreadful September day,
following their American Dream:

Patrick Adams
Leslie Arnold Austin
Rudy Bacchus
Kris Romeo Bishundauth
Pamela Boyce
Annette Datarom
Babita Guman
Nizam Hafiz
Ricknauth Jhagganauth
Charles Gregory Jolin
Bowanie Devi Kemraj
Sarab Khan
Amerdauth Luchman
Shevonne Meutis
Narendra Nath
Marcus Neblett
Hardai Parbhu
Ameena Rasool
Shiv Sankar
Sita Sewnarine
Karini Singh
Rosham Singh

Astrid Sohan
Joyce Stanton
Patricia Staton
Vanava Thompson

These are our dedicated,
hard-working country people,
who travelled from South to North
to savour just a small bite
of the Big Apple.

We will always remember them.

When September Comes

It was an ordinary September morning
just before the Autumn leaves
began to fall.
I sat horrified, speechless
in the privacy of my living room
watching the twin towers
fall.

I watched half-naked, innocent people
parachuting in panic, plunging
to escape death
only to splatter and sprawl
like shot eagles.

I watched brave, dedicated people
selflessly swarm into danger,
defying death
then taken down one by one
falling
in the line of duty.

This circumcision
at our gate,
this bleeding initiation into terror
completed a crucifixion;
painful double spear thrusts

in our side.

After witnessing
wicked deeds of wicked men,
I walked,
escaped my living room
for the green open park.

I watched chipmunks and squirrels
jump and fall so playfully
up and about the maple trees.
Clouds of white seagulls
sailing, silently circling
in our open, dangerous sky.

My faith restored,
I left the park
inhabited by God's harmless creatures,
returned to the privacy
of my living room
to reflect and compose myself.

And when September comes again
just before the Autumn leaves
begin to fall,
I will remember.

My Ajah

My Ajah, handsome, strong and proud,
was an estate-bound, cane-cutting coolie.
Banging juice for the white sahib,
from sunrise to sunset.

The hot morning sun glittered
on his aluminum saucepan,
filled with cold dhal, rice and bhajee,
which he sanayed
with his hard, cane-field fingers,
pinching a red-hot tear-me-rass pepper
as hot as the morning sun.

My Ajah, he staggered home at sunset
his sharp cutlish wrapped tightly
around the black corn bag
slung over his tired back.

Handsome, strong and proud,
he would return
the next day
to cut more cane for the white sahib,
and for the Empire,
for whom the sun never set.

Fire Fire Bun Me Haan

During our season of innocence,
cunning colonials took us away
in open steamships
dumping us on First Nations' land.

We worked for them—
setting fires to cane fields,
clearing the land.
Pricking our cotton picking fingers.
Spilling red blood
for their power and glory.

And during their season
of disruption and ruction,
they sent in the CIA
to burn down the city,
then went quietly away.

Leaving us
to set up road blocks
with firewood in the dark,
demanding jewellery
and blood money.

They taught us well
to start a fire
to hate ourselves

and destroy one another.
We must not let them off the hook,
they, who initiated a political mess
fuelled division and strife
took our hard-earned money
to build their own country,
left us in a bap,
to face all the heat and the crap.

That Terrifying Gaze

Those blue eyes of steel
melted me down
in the hot cane field,
and drove fear
in me coolie soul.

Those blue eyes of steel
would burn me up
in fields of melting snow.

But I stare back.

"Here I am!
Come now!"

For Mervyn

It was twilight
when they murdered you.
Innocent child
in the dawn of your life.

Cutting you down.
Blowing you away.
A harmless god bird—
killing you for revenge, for fun—
or out of pure hatred,
gestapo-style.

You were just following
your father.
Helping him pick up small fish,
with your tiny, harmless fingers.
Helping to feed your family.

They shot your father.
Still they were not satisfied.
So they shot you down, too.

And no one marched for you,
like they did in the town.
You were just a poor,
coolie boy
from the country.

Estate Coolie

Estate coolie
Bound for the logie
Without privacy

Estate coolie
Bound for the logie
Mek nuff picknie

Estate coolie
Bound for the logie
Drink silane pani

Estate coolie
Bound for the logie
Die from dysentery

Estate coolie
Bound for the logie
Imprisoned for truancy

Estate coolie
Bound for the logie
Wuk fu lil bit money

Estate coolie
Bound for the logie

Fight for liberty
Estate coolie
Move out of logie
Fight for respectability

Estate coolie
Is al ahbe.

Coolie Come

The cunning sahibs
and the haughty harkati
tricked, kidnapped and seduced me,
brought me across the Kalapani,
me and me jahaji.
Calling
"Come Coolie, Come!
Cheenie Chalay Coolie.
Cheenie Chalay!"

I arrived in British Guiana
on May 5th 1838.
Tired and sick
from the thrills
of the Pagla Samundar.

I walked bravely down the boardwalk
with me friendly Girmityas.
Work ethic intact,
expecting to make easy pisa.

Two different people
from continents apart,
sizing each other up—

cut eye, cut eye.

Yet, we laboured together—
foot to foot.
Cutting cane,
digging drain,
keeping out the sea.

But now, like the Harkatis,
you are kidnapping me.
Holding me hostage in Buxton.
Shooting me down in Annandale.
Demanding money and jewellery.
Baiting and beckoning:
"Come coolie come!
Coolie come!"

Khatun from Skeldon

Too tired to move about at 80,
she sits down on her steps to rest.
Once, she was the fastest, cleanest weeder,
leader of her gang.
Crop after crop,
cleaning and moulding sugar cane roots
for Booker Bros. and Company.

Now she sits
on the dung heap of estate life,
looking on, brushing flies—
abandoned by Guyanese,
by friends and family,
she laments,

 "Me prapa wuk haad, betta
weed cane root
plant garden
mine fowl
mine picknie
buy house
repair house
married picknie
now, me sid donk,
ready fu dead."

When Cheddi Died

Just as he fought the oppressors
off his people's back,
so he fought off Death,
but Death fought back.

And when Cheddi died,
the comrades at Freedom House cried.
They cried for their Comrade Leader—
The Great Freedom Fighter,
who fought the colonialists.
Who taught the poor to resist.

When Cheddi died,
the sugar workers cried.
They cried for their Labour Leader—
the Great Union Fighter,
who led the 80-day strike.
Who challenged Big Bosses for workers' rights.

When Cheddi died,
the women cried.
They cried for their Liberator,
who helped to free Kowsilla.
Crushed by a tractor,
in the heart of Leonora.

When Cheddi died,
the school children cried.
They cried for their guru,
who taught them to read.
Their modern-day Nehru,
who dispelled ignorance and greed.

When Cheddi died,
the folks on Water Street cried.
They cried for their Nation's Father,
the Great Master Builder.
Who laboured and never surrendered.
Who rebuilt a crumbling structure.

Yes, Death fought back,
putting Cheddi to rest,
but left us to continue
the fight for the oppressed.

Noisy Mornings

Brick hitting brick
Women pounding massala
Pounding pounding pounding
Grinding grinding grinding

Steel hitting steel
Men sharpening cutlish
Filing filing filing
Grinding grinding grinding

Roosters crowing
Whistle blowing
Radio blaring
Babies bawling

Calling Estate People
Calling them to rise up
Rise up!
Rise up!

Just a Drop of Ink

Jimmy bus de catridge,
fu le lil ink flow.
Dab de voting pad,
fu le de rasta go.

A simple experiment
we can't perform,
waiting and waiting
in line so long.

O when will we learn?
O when will we learn?

If we can't bus open
a pen catridge
fu lil ink, goes to show
how ahbe dese people
does tink.

How ahbe gu bus open
de interior
fu dig diamond and gold,
if all we doing
is diggin a hole?

How ahbe gu bus open
de sea,
fu all de oil
dat belong to we?

How are we going to harness
the Mighty Kaiteur,
to light up the de place,
when combackee come tour?

How long will overseer Carter
come traipsing around?
Seems like every five years
he be back in Georgetown.

Nani Goes to Vote

My Nani Painee turns out to vote.
The English-speaking returning officer asks,
"Lady, do you want to swear by the Bible?"
"Na!" Nani Painee replies.
"By the Gita?"
"Bell a wa den," Nani says, disgusted.
"Well, repeat after me," the officer says.
"I, Painee, do solemnly swear…"
"Eh Hey," murmurs Nani.
"Lady, please repeat after me."
Nani, who hardly speaks a word of English, answers
"Me dun taak am in me mine aredy."

Intellectual Arrogance

With caustic sarcasm
the minister said
"Why do you people come back here?
What do you want?"
I sat in his spacious office,
reflective and quiet,
and after a short pause,
said, "I just want to help out."
"Why don't you people stay over there?
You all have your own literacy problems.
We don't need your help."
And after a short pause,
our eyes locked.
Then for the children's sake
I pressed on:
"I just want to teach one child to read."
The minister shrugged his shoulders.
"It's up to you!"

So I went to the little village school,
and I taught the children to read.
They were happy,
the little children,
if only for a while.
And so was I.

Hindu College Days (for Carl Bassoo)

At nine o'clock,
just after the school bell rang,
we gathered to pray
in our respective ways;
then, like holy young monks,
we walked silently
to our classes.

The school buzzed
with an even humming sound
of ordinary country children
engaged in serious learning,
bathing in the freshness
of a balmy breeze
that rippled through the louvre windows
under the rough, concrete dormitory
on the lower floor.

We drank in the knowledge
dished out by a band
of self-made bramchariyas.
And I, the village boy
out of the heart
of Dafoe Battam,
turned out to Swami,
after my village play days

where I learned to sing:
"Neighba, neighba
len me yu mata du.
Me plantain cole,
e cole aready."

And so I was really out to sea
by the sea at Swamiji,
when I started to learn Hindi,
pronouncing the sacred alphabet
like a village clown.

I got nine percent
on my first Hindi test,
hiding my paper
under my desk
so no one could see.

Swamiji walked like Jesus Christ.
Sometimes fast, sometimes slow.
Jumping mud puddles
around the Ashram;
careful not to split his saffron gown,
his clean soft, brown hands
gripped tight behind his back.
Bald head, a little round belly.
Small hassar eyes
that bulged out
when he glared at you.

He knew everything
that went on around him
and when he was angry,
the whole compound froze.

He would confront you
in his thrill Indian accent:

"What are you doing here, Jailall?
How come you are not taking the Hindu Theology?"

"You see, Swami, I'm a Christian brother."

"You stupid, third class, B.G. fool.
I have big knives.
I'll kill you.
I'll suck your blood."

I trembled. How dared I?
He came to save me
from sinking deeper
into the colonial abyss
across the Kalapani.
He wanted me to remember India
with his non-sectarian Puja.

I graduated to Serious Science
at Hindu College;
Sanger Davies Lab at Q.C.

Moved to Cove & John;
there I learned that Pb means lead,
Ag silver,
and Cu copper
"Stalactites and stalagmites grow…
crystals of carbon when treated with dilute acid excrete."

The country children were taught
how to dissect crapaud.
We drowned the amphibian in formalin,
exposing the heart chambers to make it clean.

Young Ali, from Two Friends Green,
probed and demonstrated
the whole dissection scene
on Open House Night.
His muma
came to see,
and with tears in her eyes
declared,
"Aw me gawd…
look at me son,
how ya cut up crapaud!
Ya larn dacta wuk.
One day he gu cum dacta."

Working with Devotion

Estate women are full of songs
Songs to dance
Songs to work
Songs to pray

They sing the choruses
over and over,
singing along
with their tape recorder.

Women washing clothes
flinging beaters
over and over
blam blam.
Badam blam.

Women chunkaying curry
chun chun chun,
curry aroma floating,
drifting through
the morning dew.

Women washing hair
for early-morning prayer
cold water dripping,
as they stand motionless,

meditating before their altars
under the mango trees.

Women praying faithfully,
working dutifully,
as they sing
Jai Lakshmi Ramana.
Sri Lakshmi Ramana.

They sing the choruses
over and over,
singing along
with their tape recorder.

Aspects of Indrani

Indrani in Georgetown
riding her bike.
Neatly dressed in her green uniform,
books in carrier,
young Indrani looking straight ahead.

Indrani at Central Medical Lab
working with her Uncle Balwant.
Pretty girl, sweet sixteen,
taking care of business,
meeting Eddie.

Indrani with Eddie in Canada,
still neatly dressed.
Raising a family.
Standing tall, riding the subway,
going to work, punctual every day—
hard-working, never complaining.

Indrani at 50,
still with Eddie.
Spice of her family's life.
Goddess of fire, omniscient Indrani,
like the perpetual flame on Hamilton's mountain,
Her beautiful daughters carrying the torch.

Jagan & Burnham

Old men gather
in brightly-lit basements
drinking J&B whiskey
to keep themselves warm
with memory.

"A little shot
of Jagan & Burnham," they say
as they get high
talking politics,
until spit gathers
in the corners of their mouths.

And as they drink and talk,
women upstairs chat and laugh.
Baylaying dal puri
and chunkaying duck curry.

Old men get high,
they cuss and cry.
Talking more politics,
about those two chaps
who are watching from above,
laughing and knocking glasses together,
hugging up each other.
Having a grand time up there

while Guyanese cut up one another down here.

Old men's tongues tie up
as they weep and sleep,
dreaming of Jagan & Burnham
in their brightly-lit basements.
Dreaming of a home to which
they can never return
and a kind of politics
Forever gone.

A Guyanese Christmas

I remember
the Christmas Story of my childhood;
my Guyanese story of the birth
of the Christ Child.

In my young mind,
I really thought Jesus was born in Guyana
near a rice field with lots of pora,
where sheep, goats and donkeys
grazed and roamed freely.

I thought the wisemen came
from Berbice in the East,
abandoning their sheep
somewhere near Blackbush.
Followed a star
to Hope Estate on the coast,
to worship him in a real manger.

You see, you can't blame me.
I only think of Christmas in Guyana,
because Christmas anywhere else is a fake.

I remember the special Guyanese taste
of ginger beer and black cake.
of duck curry and dhal puri.

I remember the carol singing
in Ann's Grove Village Church,
the village masquerade
brightening up the place.
Buck Shea and Wallace our leading musicians,
waving their hankies in the air—
red Hankies that were once
our banners of peace.

I remember the toys
that brought me pleasure,
long before the Internet and TV.
A soft, green bumper ball,
a white whistle
with a spinning global cork,
a big red balloon.
I squeezed the air out at the neck
to entertain myself,
and when it burst
I made red cherries,
rubbing them gleefully
on my palm.

Here in the big city
we do not see a real cow or a donkey.
We just sit and stare and watch TV,
pretending to be happy.

We have drifted from what's real.
Forgotten the Christmas story.
The true meaning of the season
already stolen
by the dazzling lights
in lonely shopping malls.

We must switch off
those artificial lights
and look to the light within.
To the light Baby Jesus brought into the world,
to the light he brought to Guyana,
that once shone so brightly
when we were young.

The Ole Country

When I visit the ole country
I don't ask for much—
just a small sal bag,
a few Buxton spice,
and a glass of frothy mauby
with a piece of ice.

The Moon

When the electricity cuts out,
the music stops.
Darkness blankets the land,
and the lantern of the night
casts a natural light.

Children play kakadeelo,
running through golden moonbeams,
while the glittering coconut branches sway.
A solitary moon pass coconut falls,
swearing at it,
for making it barren.

But the lantern of the night
sails on majestically;
among the powdery clouds,
above the towering coconut trees.
Enduring praises and curses.
Never fading out.

Mother Bird

When morning breaks,
Mother Bird peeps out.
Flits about her embroidered nest,
bathing her yellow breast
in the rainbow rays
that criss-cross the shimmering leaves
of the old hibiscus tree.

I know Mother Bird
by her instinctive morning call;
distinguished, soothing,
gentle and precise—
nature's morning clock.

So wake me up, Mother Bird.
Clear your throat
and sing me a song
to start this new-born day,
from your secret spot,
deep inside the green thicket
of the old hibiscus tree.

Travelling Through the Woods

Poling along
skimming through the sweet black water
travelling through the woods.
Poling along
skimming through the sweet black water
that tumbles down the Mighty Amazon.
Mindful of vicious piranhas,
I sink the pole deep in the sand and clay,
pushing on the alluvial plain,
heading toward the hilly sand and clay belt.
Gripping my smooth bamboo pole,
I count wild fruit trees as I go,
hard white trunks supporting
bunches of heavy purple jamoon
with fat juicy veins.
I share the sweet wine with a flock
of fast-flying jittery blue saki.
I savour sumutoo soup,
sucking, pulling in the seeds.
I share yellow mangoes
with screeching parakeets.
I burst a star apple,
to drink from the dripping star.
I open two guavas,
chocolate and white ladies,
checking first for worms.
I peel a prickly pineapple

with my sharp grass knife,
to cleanse my stomach.
I feast on fruits with birds and beasts,
as I travel through the tropical woods,
poling along in my sturdy bateau
as I go,
working on the farm.

Trying to Catch Nature

The speed boat flies
down the sleepy creek,
waking up
the sacred Canje pheasant
the green parrots
screaming
the white-masked monkeys
jeering with red gums.

Nature so difficult to embrace
keeps flying in your face.

After Life

When this breath is gone
and I retire in a lovely sleep,
I'll be in a far-away place,
dreaming peacefully
in the loving arms
of my creator God.

So please remember me
whenever you see
that sweet smile on the face
of a child,
or the radiance
of a beautiful sunset.

You will hear me when
you visit the ole country;
listen for my voice,
singing joyfully
amid the mist
of the waterfall.

When this breath is gone
and all that's left is my soul,
my spirit will soar
among those gone before,
until it finds
its final resting place.

Two Umbrella Trees

On the first day of spring,
when the buds appear,
we are out
working side by side,
pruning two umbrella trees,
which shelter a pair of doves.

We pull down dead wood,
exposing the younger shoots,
making the old trees new again.

Hoping the doves return.

Walking on Dams

Walking barefoot on mud dam.
Clay squelching between my toes,
the strong smell
of chunkayed curry
knocking me down.

Walking on line dam.
Lifting the red cap
off the sweetie bush;
sharing the nectar
with humming birds.

Walking along bamboo dam.
Plucking dry seeds
from the tulsie bush, rubbing
and inhaling the fragrance
of my youth.

It's Not Easy

After 33 long years,
it's not easy to leave
the Beautiful Garden,
where I've greeted the world
each morning
at the school gate.

After reading little Emma's farewell letter—
"Dear Mr. Jailall:
thank you
for helping me learn things
I will miss you plenty. Good bye"—
It's not easy to leave.

After the philistines moved in,
tried to destroy the Beautiful Garden,
served us sour grapes
and rotten apples,
it's still not easy
to separate us from Emma.

Rocking in my Hammock

Rocking gently, half-covered
in my bottom house hammock;
feet outstretched
hands gripped behind my neck.
Looking out,
watching and rocking,
eyes glancing where the streets intersect
to see the universe of the estate spin.

People hustling for a living

Sellers of coconut brooms.
Sellers of coconut buns.
Sellers of coconuts.
Sellers of fish and bread.

Little children walking briskly
to the cake shops.
Women running
to catch the market.
Cane cutters bathed in black dust,
hurrying home to wash.
A minibus with a heavy load,
jerking home in the sunset.
A dog chasing a cow.

A drunk stumbling out of a rum shop,
singing.
I continue to rock,

as the Estate spins.

Exercising in Georgetown

Georgetown at 5 a.m.
Rima Guest House.
I'm heading for the Seawall Bandstand,
neatly dressed
in my foreign jogging suit.

The youths are up, too,
at Middle & Main.
Watching.
Nothing to do
but stand and stare.

Grey hair, middle-aged
foreign-looking man.
Walking briskly,
arms swinging.
They smile.

I pass the landmarks
of my youth.
The old rail station
once filled with smoke and soot,
with chugging engines,
whistles that shrieked
and men in uniform.

I pass the CIDA House,
where Canadians scatter seed money
like yellow rice paddy.

I pass the Church House,
where priests work tirelessly
with the wretched of the Earth.

I pass the Red House,
once feared
because of its colour.

I pass Youmana Yana,
exotic and local,
a native meeting place.

I pass the embassies,
American and Canadian—
gateways to the land of opportunities.

Before the foreign hotel
the soldiers pound
the clean pavement.
Left right left right.

I run…

to the ancient bandstand
where the police choir once sang.

A few street people are asleep;
some already waking,
bathing in the breeze of the early-morning sea.

A jogger calls out to me—
a Canadian combackee I know.
We talk and walk,
casting our eyes on the horizon,
far, far away.

I turn around,
start my return run.
It's 6 a.m.
I insert the key in the brass lock,
on the Rima Guest House door.
Slowly, I turn
time, like the hands
of the Stabroek Clock,
trying to unlock
an unknown city—

entering as a stranger.
A foreigner in a foreign place,
with people watching me.

High Tide

When high tide comes in
it brings white birds
drenched in oil,
staggering on Tar Beach.

High tech comes in with high tide
sweeping up baby fish
drenched in oil,
tossing them on Tar Beach.

When high tide comes in
people just stand and stare,
folding their arms,
watching on Tar Beach.

Healing Water

Land of Water,
many waters,
cool running water
running everywhere.
Healing water always there.
But not in Buxton,
where terrorists hide,
ready to kill
anyone
who dares to enter.

Land of Water,
many waters,
cool running water
running every where.
Healing water always there.
But not in Omai,
where strangers always dig,
hot poison flowing
down the Mighty River.

Land of Water,
many waters,
cool running water,
running everywhere.
Healing water always there.

But not in Georgetown
where everything is broken down.

Land of Water,
many waters,
cool running water,
running everywhere.

Healing water
always there.

The Fruit Seller

Sumintra sits patiently
on her wooden peerha
under the spreading neem tree,
near Mahaica big bridge,
where the river bends
and the road curves,
selling the best tropical fruits
grown in the land.

Smooth, round, brown sapodillas.
Short, sweet, yellow fig bananas.
White and purple star apples,
juice running down you elbows me buddy.
Rattling green avocados.
Yellow spice mangoes.
Beautiful red cashews,
insides white like candy floss.
Huge watermelons sounding,
kangsing sweeter than tassa drumming.

Sumintra awaits the arrival
of the minibus and the speedboat
on the other side of the world,
far away from the Big Market.

Blackout

The flies hover around
the dirty light bulb
in this hot country.
Suddenly the radio stops
and a child begins to cry.

"Blackout!" announces a disappointed neighbour.

I feel my way around the house,
groping in the dark,
gripping walls, tables, chairs, banister—
hungry for a ray of light, a match.

Rain falls.

Then a flash of lightning.
Thunder rolls;
dogs bark and donkeys bray.
Mother Nature is disturbed,

and even God is angry at us.

Iron Works

Iron bars decorate windows
doors and verandas.
Padlocks hug iron gates.
Heavy keys dangle on sweaty bodies,
weighing them down

Guard dogs tug on thick chains.
Fluorescent lights burn in the pitch-dark.
Security sleeps under big houses

as bandits rule the night.

Poet's Work

We talk straight
when we don't talk in parables,
cutting through the muck
of circumlocution.

We use words to paint
on the canvas of the mind,
designing the textures of life.

Our words cause sharp stirrings
in the chambers of the heart.

We bless
We curse
We praise
We blame
We name

That's when we talk straight,
and not in parables.

I Can't Go Home

I want to go home
but I can't go home.
I'm afraid of the terrorists
pointing guns.

I want to go home
but I can't go home.
I'm afraid of the terrorists
blindfolding me.

I want to go home
but I can't go home.
I'm afraid to sleep
when the place gets dark.

So I'm staying right here,
in my peaceful Canadian home,
where I can go to sleep
with an open door.

Killing Machines

The Big Bad Boys
make killing machines.
Not in ammunition factories,
but with other people's children.

Teaching them acts of patriotism;
serving King and Country,
then sending them out
to kill
or be killed,
with heavy weapons
and fast jet planes.

Teaching them to use
the Language of War

to justify murder.

What My Father Taught Me

Long before the red tractor
was imported from Canada
I followed in the furrows
of my father's wooden plough,
walking behind him through the rice field mud.

My father used his nation language,
coaxing the tired oxen:
"Dahin!
Ah Ah Ah
Ah He Ah
Dahin!"

And when the oxen were going straight,
he burst into song,
"Ginee Ginee Taray!"
And as he sang he looked up
longingly
at the beautiful tropical sky.

I learned the rice field language
in my native village,
hoping to pass it on
to my Canadian children.

So when I settled
in the land of the red tractor,

and I pushed a green lawn mower
while my children followed me
with their lawn mower toys,

I had forgotten
the rice field language,

and my father's song.

I Thought I was a Guyanese

All my life,
I thought I was a Guyanese.
I was born there.
My parents were born there.
And my grandparents were born there, too.

I eat garlic pork and konkey,
prasad and curry,
cassava bread and pone.
I eat labba
and drink creekwater.
I even drink Blackman juta,
sipping from the same communion cup,
at Camp Street Brethren Church.

I thought I was a Guyanese
until one day,
when I dared to walk alone
under the old Stabroek market clock.

Three young black boys
armed with sticks and knives
surrounded me, asking,
"Where is de money?
Where is de fuckin money?
Coolie gat plenty money

Give we de money!"
I looked them straight in the eye
and asked,

"Where are your parents?
Where are your elders?
Why are you cussing?
Why are you not at school?"

Den me hempty me packit.
"Heh, tek money."
Me push am in dem face.
And from then I knew—

a coolie is always a coolie.

Letter to Kamala-Jean

Like you,
I wanted details.

The name of the ship.
The meaning of my name.
The origin of my ancestors. Details
of their punishment, humiliation,
death.
Knowledge
of how they were treated,
of how they were hated.

Children jeered:

"Coolie Gal! Your ancestors
arrived at Port Royal
with tails like monkeys
which had to be cut off"

Taunted,
labelled:

"Coolie Gal
fit only to sell Callaloo
on Spanish Town Road"

You are
Jamaican
East Indian
West Indian
Indo-Caribbean

Canadian.

Like you, I am not only East-Indian—
I'm Guyanese, Caribbean and Canadian,
visible with a voice.
We have many identities

Now I know
no more Coolie Gal,
but dignified woman—
intelligent
and strong.

Second Migration

Aware of my traditional ways
from peasantry,
my tech-savvy son
navigated the net,
surfing for a suitable hotel.
"Good price!" he announced joyfully.

The next day,
we drove 500 miles
in the white winter rain
to the Holiday Inn,
in Philadelphia.

His head held high,
he stepped confidently
into the waiting elevator.

"Welcome to bourgeois living, dad!" he teased.
"It's lovely," I replied,
then reminded him
of Dorothy's longing for Kansas.

"There's no place like home."

The ancestral home,
My Son.

About the Author

Peter Jailall, a teacher, poet and storyteller, was born in Guyana in 1944. He is the author of two previous books of poetry: *This Healing Place* (1993) and *Yet Another Home* (1997). Peter is a member of the Racial Minority Writer's Collective and the League of Canadian Poets. He has read his poetry in schools, libraries and universities across North America, the United Kingdom, the Caribbean and Guyana. An avid supporter of human rights and social justice, he expresses his compassion and passion for human values through his poetry. He was a finalist in the 2002 Mississauga Arts Award in the category of Established Literary Artist. Peter lives in Mississauga with his wife, Sabi, and their two sons, Dave and Nari.